# A is for Anaconda

## A Rainforest Alphabet

Written by Anthony D. Fredericks and Illustrated by Laura Regan

Text Copyright © 2009 Anthony D. Fredericks
Illustration Copyright © 2009 Laura Regan

Sleeping Bear Press™
2395 South Huron Parkway, Suite 200
Ann Arbor, MI 48104
www.sleepingbearpress.com


Printed and bound in the United States.

10 9 8 7 6 5 4

Library of Congress Cataloging-in-Publication Data

Fredericks, Anthony D.
A is for anaconda : a rainforest alphabet / written by Anthony D.
Fredericks ; illustrated by Laura Regan.
p. cm.
Summary: "Using the alphabet book format the rainforest is explored
and explained. A poem explains each topic followed by detailed
expository text. Topics include Brazil, epiphytes, gorillas, Kapok tree
and nocturnal" —Provided by publisher.
ISBN 978-1-58536-317-9
1. Rain forest animals—Juvenile literature. 2. Alphabet books.
I. Regan, Laura, ill. II. Title.
QL112.F73 2009
591.734--dc22                                        2008037600

*For Camryn Ohl: Wishing you fantastic discoveries,*
*incredible adventures, and many magical journeys!*

A. D. F.

✿

*For my first grandchild, J.Z., with lots of love!*

L. R.

# A a

Watch out! Look closely and you'll see one of the longest snakes in the world—the powerful anaconda. A full grown anaconda snake can be very big. The longest recorded anaconda was 28 feet (8.5 m) long. That's longer than a car! That specimen had a girth of 44 inches (112 cm) and weighed nearly 500 pounds (227 kg). Anacondas belong to a group of snakes known as constrictors. When they capture their prey, they wrap their bodies around the victim and slowly squeeze—tighter and tighter. The victim is unable to breathe and eventually suffocates. Then, the anaconda unhinges its jaw and swallows the victim whole. Anacondas have been known to swallow large animals such as deer and jaguars. They are frequently found in the rainforests of South America.

**A** also stands for Australia. Australian rainforests are home to some of the most distinctive animals and plants in the world. Although some of Australia's rainforests have been destroyed by burning, road building, and real estate development, many are protected in state and national parks.

A is for Anaconda,
    its size—a scary feature.
It swims and slips through rivers deep,
    and eats most any creature.

# Bb

B is for Brazil,
  a land both wild and free—
the Amazon winds through it,
  from the Andes to the sea.

Brazil is the largest country in South America. It is over 3,300,000 square miles (8,500,000 sq km)—the United States is 3,500,000 square miles (9,300,000 sq km) and Canada is 3,800,000 square miles (9,400,000 sq km). More than 172 million people live in Brazil. Consisting of dense forests, semiarid scrub land, rugged mountains, rolling plains, and a long coastal strip, Brazil's landmass is dominated by the Amazonian rainforest. The Amazon River, which is more than 4,000 miles (6,400 km) long, flows eastward through Brazil and empties into the Atlantic Ocean.

Bromeliads begin with **B**. These are plants that grow in both the understory and canopy layers of the rainforest. They live on the branches and trunks of many trees. They have developed a unique way of obtaining water and nutrients. Most bromeliads have long curved leaves that overlap at the base forming a tight bowl at the bottom. This bowl collects falling rainwater, sometimes as much as 2 gallons (7.58 liters). These pools of water are home to many varieties of animals such as frogs, insects, worms, and spiders.

The canopy layer is one of the four layers of the tropical rainforest. From bottom to top the layers include the forest floor, the understory (a dark layer with slow-growing plants), the canopy, and the emergent layer (which includes the heads of the tallest trees—those 200 feet [61 m] tall or more). Filled with sights, sounds, and colors, the canopy layer of the rainforest is truly amazing. Most of the animals and plants of the rainforest live in this layer. Swinging monkeys, swooping birds, climbing frogs, and lazy sloths make their way through the thick vegetation. Here, the trees are 65 to 100 feet (20 to 30 m) tall.

Chicle [CHEE-kluh] also starts with **C**. Chicle is the gum from the chicle tree, a tropical evergreen tree. For years it was used as the basic ingredient in chewing gum. It was harvested in much the same way as latex is tapped from rubber trees. Today chewing gum is made from artificial ingredients rather than chicle.

C is for the Canopy,
   a layer filled with sounds
of squawking birds and monkeys wild—
   a place where life abounds.

Dispersers are animals that scatter plant seeds throughout the rainforest. Many creatures live on a diet of tropical fruits, including the seeds. As these animals travel through the forest, they disperse, or spread, the seeds with their wastes. The seeds often grow into new plants, thus ensuring the survival of the plant species as well as the diversity of life in this fragile ecosystem. There are various kinds of dispersers in the rainforest. These may include bats, monkeys, insects, and a wide range of mammals such as tapirs, agoutis, and lemurs. In most rainforests, birds are the primary seed dispersers.

**D** is also for deforestation. Once, rainforests covered about 14 percent of the earth's surface; today they cover a mere 6 percent. Most rainforests are cleared for their timber. The loss of trees—deforestation—has a significant impact on many animal species. Most rainforests are cleared using chainsaws, bulldozers, and fires. Unbelievably, more than 200,000 acres (80,000 ha) of rainforest are burned every day—that's 78 million acres (31 million ha) every year! Some scientists estimate that at the current rate of deforestation, the world's remaining rainforests could be consumed in less than 50 years.

D is for Dispersers
who eat and spread the seeds.
They help the forest thrive,
providing for its needs.

E is for the Epiphytes
that grow among the trees.
They get their water from the air,
and flutter in the breeze.

An epiphyte [EP-uh-fite] is a plant that grows on the branches or trunks of other plants. These rainforest plants typically have no roots; they take their food and water from the surrounding atmosphere. In short, these plants do not need soil to grow and thrive. Epiphytes are also known as air plants since they grow so high in the trees. Some epiphytes have roots that absorb water right from the air and some are able to store water in a small cup in the center of the plant. They obtain nutrients from litter that falls from the trees or the dust dissolved in rainwater. Some mosses and ferns are epiphytes.

Endangered also begins with **E**. An endangered species is one that is in danger of dying out completely, never to return (known as *extinction*). When a plant or animal is extinct, it has ceased to survive forever. Some scientists estimate that thousands of rainforest plant and animal species are endangered.

# Ff

F is for the Food web
of animals and plants.
They all are linked together
like falcons ➠ frogs ➠ and ants.

The organisms in a rainforest are linked together through a series of feeding relationships. Plants use energy from the sun to produce food. The food is eaten by some animals, providing the energy they need to survive. These animals may be eaten by other (usually larger) animals. In turn, those animals are eaten by another group of (even larger) animals. This series is known as a food chain. Here's an example:

*sun ➠ bananas ➠ monkey ➠ harpy eagle*

It might look like the consumption of one organism by another happens in a straight line. However, nature is never that simple. Several organisms may be involved at several different levels, each dependent on several others for its food supply. Since most rainforest organisms eat more than one type of food, most organisms belong to more than one food chain. When several chains are combined they form a food web. In other words, every plant and animal is dependent on every other plant and animal to live and to survive.

G is for Gorillas.
In territories green,
they eat and sleep and live their lives,
and are seldom ever seen.

There are two species of gorillas—the Western Gorilla and the Eastern Gorilla. Most gorillas live in western Africa. The western lowland gorilla and the eastern lowland gorilla both live in the tropical rainforests of Cameroon, Central African Republic, Gabon, Congo, Equatorial Guinea, and Zaire. Even though they are large and look mean, gorillas are quite shy and very gentle. They forage for leaves, herbs, stems, and vines, but don't stay long enough in one area to exhaust the food supply. They form stable family groups in sizes ranging from five individuals up to several dozen members. They communicate using grunts, howls, roars, and hooting. Scientists estimate that there are only 50,000 gorillas left in the wild.

**G** is for Geckos. These amazing creatures have special toes with thousands of micro-scopic hair-like bristles. This allows the gecko to walk on any surface, including upside down on branches. The incredible flying gecko has flaps of leathery skin that allow it to glide from tree to tree to escape danger.

There are more than 300 species of humming-birds—most of which live in the rainforests of South America. With brilliant colors and iridescent hues, these tiny creatures (from 2 to 8½ inches [5 to 22 cm] long) dart and dance through the trees. These birds were revered by the ancient Aztecs who believed that every warrior slain in battle eventually became a hummingbird. Most hummingbirds flap their wings about 50 times a second. Because of a fast breathing rate and a rapid heartbeat (up to 1,260 times a minute) they must feed every 10 minutes or so. Interestingly, a humming-bird can fly forward, backward, and upside down—but it cannot walk.

**H** is also for the Harpy Eagle. These creatures are some of the largest and most powerful birds of prey in the world. They are about 3 feet (1 m) long with a wingspan of 6 feet (2 m). They live in the rainforests of Central and South America where they hunt sloths, monkeys, large reptiles, and other birds.

H h

H is for the Hummingbird,
a teeny little critter,
with feathers iridescent—
they sparkle and they glitter.

# I i

I is for Iguana,
a creature big and bold.
It climbs up trees and swims through streams,
and lives to be quite old.

Iguanas, mostly green iguanas, live through-out the tropical rainforest, primarily along river banks. They usually weigh between 10 to 15 pounds (4.5 to 6.8 kg), although some can reach weights of up to 40 pounds (18 kg). Most will grow to lengths of 6 or 7 feet (1.8 to 2.1 m) with a serrated crest along their back. Primarily herbivores (plant eaters), they live on a diet of fruit, flowers, and leaves, although they occasionally eat insects and other small animals. Their legs are long and powerful and they can run quickly for short distances. They have been known to live up to 20 years when in captivity.

Insectivore also begins with I. Insectivores are animals that live primarily on a diet of insects. Rainforest insectivores include frogs, anteaters, lizards, birds, and snakes. There are many thousands of species of ants as well as tens of thousands of beetle species in the rainforest. As you might imagine, there are lots of insectivores around to eat all those bugs!

# J j

J is for Jaguars
who sneak across the ground.
They lurk in bushes, hide in trees,
and hardly make a sound.

Jaguars are wild cats that live throughout Central and South America. These graceful creatures usually inhabit dense rainforest areas—somewhere near a swampy area or beside a river (they are excellent swimmers). Their home range can vary from 2 to 200 square miles (5 to 500 sq km), depending on the availability of food. They grow up to six feet (1.8 m) long with broad heads and extremely powerful paws. Fierce predators, they live on a diet of monkeys, rodents, deer, turtles, fish, frogs, and birds. They often bury their prey after killing it, in order to eat it later. They are solitary animals and hunt mostly at night.

**J** is for the "Jesus Christ" lizard (also known as the green basilisk lizard). When these creatures are disturbed by an enemy, they drop out of the trees where they live into the water below. Extremely fast runners, they are able to scamper across the surface of a pond or stream without falling in. Hence, their nickname.

K is for the Kapok tree—
its buttressed roots spread wide.
With this support the tree stands tall,
and creatures hunt and hide.

K k

Kapok trees can be found in rainforests throughout the world. Since kapok trees can be more than 100 feet (30 m) tall and 10 feet (3 m) in diameter, they have large spreading roots, known as buttresses, that support them. These buttresses are large enough for animals to hide in or build their nests. The trees flower during the flood season and produce special fruit pods. These pods contain lightweight, water-resistant fibers known as kapok which is similar to cotton. This material is used as a filling for life jackets and pillows, as well as for insulating walls.

**K** is for Kinkajou. Kinkajous are small, nocturnal animals that are closely related to raccoons. They are omnivores—they will eat almost anything, including honey, fruit, insects, small mammals, and birds. They use their very long, narrow tongues to obtain honey from beehives or nectar from tropical flowers. Their prehensile [pree-HEN-sil] tail, which acts like a grasping hand, helps them swing from branch to branch as they scurry through the rainforest.

L is for the Litter
that cascades night and day.
It falls upon the forest floor
to crumble, rot, decay.

Litter is all the dead leaves, seeds, flowers, and other plant material that falls onto the forest floor. This material falls constantly through night and day and helps form part of the soil. Interestingly, almost five tons (10,000 pounds [4500 kg]) of litter may fall on the rainforest floor in just one year. There it begins to quickly rot and decay. This occurs through the action of fungi, termites, and other organisms. This action creates a rich layer of humus. The humus is home to thousands of different types of creatures— from skittering reptiles to creepy-crawly bugs.

**L** is for Leaf Cutter Ants. These creatures live below ground in enormous nests with more than 5 million residents. Each day they set off to strip trees of their leaves, shoots, and stems. They carry these pieces back to their underground chambers where they chew them up into compost. On the compost they grow a special fungus which is used for food.

L l

For thousands of years, people of the rainforest have been using plants to cure diseases and heal illnesses. Native peoples have used rainforest plants to treat arthritis, heal snake bites, and cure skin infections. They have discovered the miraculous medicines available from rainforest plants and are now sharing that knowledge with doctors worldwide. In fact, some people have called the rainforest the "world's medicine chest" because of its potential for curing diseases such as cancer, AIDS, and influenza. Interestingly, more than 100 prescription drugs sold worldwide have their origins in rainforest plants. One of the reasons why there are so many medicines found in the rainforest is simply because of the wide variety of plants there. Many of those plants have developed chemicals to protect them from being eaten by insects and other animals. While those chemicals may be distasteful or deadly to rainforest animals, they may be quite helpful to humans in curing specific diseases or treating life-threatening illnesses.

M
m

M is for the Medicines
   we've looked for hard and long.
They cure, protect, and heal us,
   and help to keep us strong.

# N n

Nocturnal animals are active at night and rest or sleep during daylight hours. Diurnal animals are those active during the day. Nocturnal rainforest animals often have special adaptations that help them survive in the dark. For example, lemurs, geckos, and the red-eyed tree frog have special eyes that see well in very dim light. Various species of bats use echolocation, in which they emit a high-pitched sound that bounces off objects. The sound is then received by the bat, giving it information about the object's shape, direction, and distance. Some animals, like fruit bats, use a highly developed sense of smell to locate food in the darkness.

New Guinea begins with **N**. This country is located just above Australia and is the world's second largest island. It has one of the most diverse collections of rainforest animals anywhere—200,000 species of insects, up to 20,000 plant species, 650 bird species, 400 amphibians, 455 butterfly species, and nearly 300 species of mammals.

N is for Nocturnal—
the creatures of the night,
who hunt for food throughout the dark,
and are hidden from our sight.

O is for the Orchids,
    great beauty everywhere—
a world of flashy species,
    each one beyond compare!

In the tropical rainforest there are more than 25,000 different species of orchids. Orchids, like many other flowers, depend on insects for their pollination. As a result, these flowers have evolved into a wide range of distinctive shapes, brilliant colors, and incredible patterns. Many orchids blossom in an upside-down position relative to the stem. About 50 percent of all orchids are epiphytes—they are not rooted in the ground, but grow on other plants.

**O** is for Okapi. Relatives of the giraffe, these creatures live in the rainforests of western Africa. They have dark brown heads and bodies, but the stripes on their legs are similar to those of a zebra. They use their long tongues to obtain leaves and fruits from trees.

Orangutans, an endangered rainforest species, begins with **O**. These playful creatures, which live in Sumatra and Borneo, are especially fond of eating fruits. They are considered highly intelligent because of their ability to use tools.

Oo

P—Poison Dart Frogs,
in red or orange or black.
Their colors are to warn you,
"Watch out!" or "Stand back!"

Poison dart frogs live in the rainforests of Central and South America. They come in a rainbow of colors including brown, green, red, orange, yellow, blue, and black. Some have stripes or dots on their bodies. There are over one hundred different kinds of poison dart frogs and most are smaller than your big toe. In spite of their small size, they are some of the most dangerous animals anywhere. That's because when they get scared or excited, deadly poisons are released through their skin. These poisons are powerful enough to harm or kill many other animals—including humans.

**P** is for one of the most infamous fish in the world—the Piranha. Piranhas are native to freshwater streams and lakes throughout South America. They are ferocious carnivores that often attack amphibians, rodents, and birds in the water. They range from one-half to two feet (15 to 60 cm) in length and have many razor-sharp teeth. Don't get too close!

P p

Quetzals [ket-SALZ] are some of the most beautiful birds in the rainforest. With a scarlet belly and bright green feathers over most of its body, this bird is a rare sight to see. Most noticeable are its 2 to 3 foot (60 to 90 cm) long emerald tail feathers (twice as long as its body). These feathers were prized by the Aztecs and used for elaborate headdresses worn by tribal chiefs. To the ancient Mayas, the quetzal represented wealth because they were rare. Quetzal feathers, along with jade, were their most sought after treasures. People in Guatemala revere the quetzal so much that they chose it as their national bird, and even named their currency the "quetzal." Unfortunately there are so few of these birds remaining that they are considered an endangered species.

Quinine [KWY-nine] also begins with **Q**. Quinine is a drug made from the bark of the cinchona tree. This medicine has been used by rainforest natives for hundreds of years to treat malaria, a deadly tropical disease. Worldwide, over 200 million people are affected by malaria.

**Q** is for the Quetzal—
an Aztec word, "of beauty."
With feathers green and bellies red,
it is a sight to see!

**R** is for the constant Rain
that falls throughout the year.
It keeps the forest soaking wet
and the air both clean and clear.

# R r

The rainforest is called a rainforest for one simple reason—lots and lots of rain. The average tropical rainforest gets about 80 inches (203 cm) of rain a year—that's more than 1 inch (about 3 cm) every week. Some rainforests in South America get as much as 400 inches (1016 cm) every year. In most climates, evaporated rainfall is carried away to fall as rain in distant areas. But in the tropical rainforest, 50 percent of the precipitation comes from its own evaporation. Interestingly, much of the rain that falls on the rainforest never reaches the ground. It stays on the trees because the leaves act as a shield.

**R** is for Red-eyed Tree Frogs. These big-eyed creatures (who can see in very dim light) can be found clinging to branches and leaves with suction-tipped toes. They often live their whole lives in the trees and never come down to the ground.

One of the most unusual animals in the world, the sloth spends almost its entire life upside down. It not only walks upside down through the rainforest trees, it also sleeps, mates, and gives birth to its babies while it hangs upside down. There are two different species of sloths—the two-toed sloth and the three-toed sloth. Sloths can easily hide in the branches of rainforest trees because their hair is often covered by a thin layer of green algae. Their green color and sluggish habits make these creatures look more like masses of leaves than living animals.

**S** is also for South America. Most of the world's rainforests can be found in South America. Here, the average temperature does not vary by more than 15 degrees (10 degrees Celsius) throughout the entire year. The typical range of temperature may be as high as 90°F (33°C) or as low as 75°F (23°C). The Equator runs right through South America.

S s

S is for the Sloth.
Like an acrobatic clown,
it spends its days and nights
in a world that's upside down.

# T t

T is for Tarantula,
a fuzzy little beast.
The largest one eats birds and bats—
a most delicious feast!

Tarantulas are scary-looking creatures. Long hairy legs, a frightful face, and enormous fangs make this rainforest spider one of the most feared in the world. There are about 650 species, primarily in tropical and sub-tropical countries. The largest tarantula in the world is the goliath bird-eating spider of South America. This rainforest spider weighs up to four ounces (113 gm) and has an 11-inch (28 cm) leg span—about the size of a dinner plate. It eats baby birds, rats, frogs, small snakes, and lizards (but never any students).

Topsoil begins with **T**. Rainforest soil is quite different from the soil in your back-yard. Rainforest soil is filled with an abundance of organic life, yet it is very thin. High temperatures, high humidity, and many microorganisms in the soil contribute to a very rapid decomposition process. As a result, not many nutrients are available for plants to use. Many rainforest plants must be deep-rooted in order to obtain the nutri-ents needed for survival.

The uakari [wah-KAHR-ee] is a medium-sized rainforest monkey. There are two species—the red or bald uakari and the black uakari. They live throughout Brazil, Colombia, and Peru. Uakaris are diurnal and are often found in the tops of large trees. Their diet consists mainly of a variety of fruits, but they will also eat leaves, seeds, insects, and small animals. They usually search for food in small groups, but will gather in troops of up to 50 individuals in the evening. The deforestation of the rainforest is eliminating many of the trees in which this creature lives.

Uanano also begins with **U**. The Uanano are an indigenous (native) rainforest people who live in the river basins of Brazil and Colombia. Only about 1600 Uananos remain today. They survive mainly through fishing and gardening. Interestingly, they prohibit the cutting of trees near the river because they fear a resulting decline in the fish population.

U u

Uakari starts with U.
They eat most any fruit,
and often swing among the trees.
Their face is almost cute.

The spice we know as vanilla comes from the world's largest orchid plant. Vanilla orchids form on vines that grow up tree trunks. The greenish yellow flowers produce a bean that creates the distinctive vanilla odor and taste. The beans are air-dried for several months. Then, the cured beans are crushed and the flavors extracted with alcohol and water. The vanilla flavoring is used in ice cream, cookies, and other bakery products. Vanilla vines have been grown by humans for thousands of years, and the island nation of Madagascar is now the largest producer (3 million metric tons) of vanilla in the world.

Vine snakes begin with **V**. These long, thin snakes inhabit the rainforests of Central and South America. Growing to a length of six feet (1.8 m) they blend easily into the tropical landscape—looking like just another part of a tree or plant. Their diet consists mainly of small lizards and mammals.

V v

V is for Vanilla,
a spice we love to eat.
It flavors ice cream, cookies, cakes—
the taste just can't be beat!

Walking sticks are one of about 3,000 species of stick insects that live throughout the world—many of them in tropical regions. They are members of a family of insects with the scientific name *Phasmidae*. This is a Greek word that means "apparition" (ghost or phantom). These creatures are extremely thin, with long, spindly legs and compressed bodies. Some types can grow to be 13 inches (33 cm) long! Typically they are green or brown so that they look exactly like a twig, stick, or plant stem. In fact, all their body parts resemble plant parts. When they walk, these curious creatures look like moving twigs. When they stand still, which they do quite often, they look like an extension of a branch or stick. If captured, the walking stick can break off one of its own legs—leaving an attacker with a very small body part to eat. The walking stick later grows a new leg.

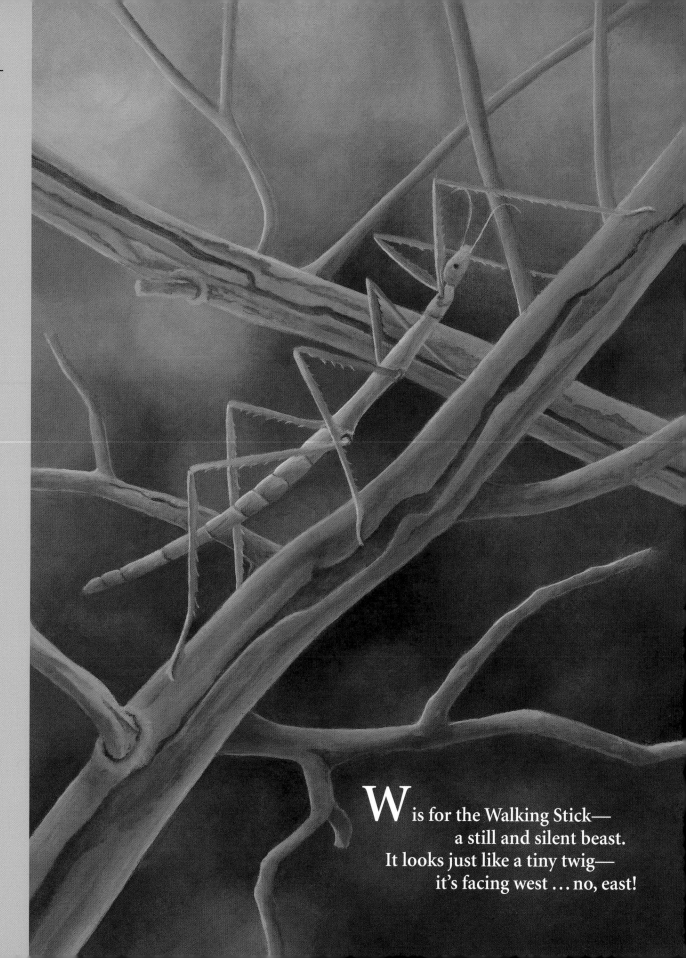

W is for the Walking Stick—
a still and silent beast.
It looks just like a tiny twig—
it's facing west ... no, east!

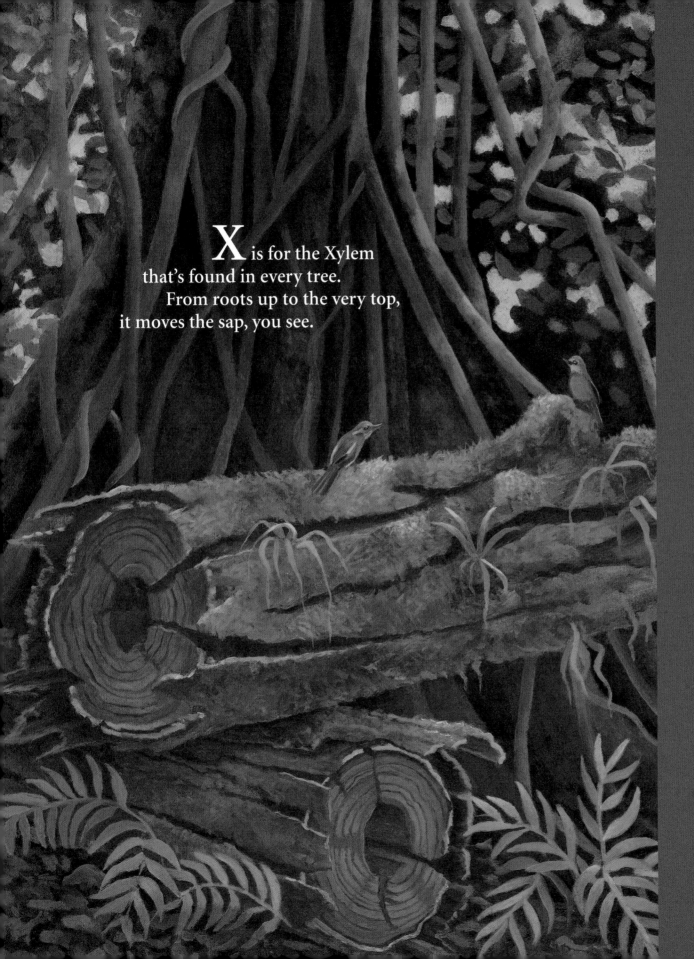

# X

**X** is for the Xylem
that's found in every tree.
From roots up to the very top,
it moves the sap, you see.

Xylem [ZY-lum] is a series of vessels, or tubes, that are found in many kinds of woody plants, including trees. These vertical tubes, just like drinking straws, move water from the roots of a plant up to its leaves. Sap, a combination of water and nutrients from the soil, also moves up the xylem to feed the plant. The xylem also takes part in food storage and support for the plant. It's the xylem that is able to move water and minerals from the tips of the roots up to the top of 200-foot (60 m) rainforest trees.

**X** is also for Xenops [ZEN-ops]. This is a small (about 5 inches [12 cm] long) rainforest bird that lives from southern Mexico down through northern Argentina. Xenops usually like to live in dead or decaying trees lined with grass and other plant materials. Their diet consists of ants and other small insects. It pounds a piece of decaying wood with its bill and eats the insects that crawl out.

Yanomamo starts with **Y**—
a people proud and free.
Among the creatures and the plants,
they live in harmony.

The Yanomamo people live in central Brazil—an environment they have inhabited for thousands of years. They exist in almost complete seclusion—having no contact with people outside the rainforest. Living in small tribes, they spend much of their daily life gardening, hunting, and making crafts. Although they have no written language, they have developed a complex system of trading between tribes. Each tribe has a chief who is responsible for the safety of tribal members as well as for preserving the general knowledge of the surrounding environment. Their primitive way of life and their territory, however, are being lost along with the elimination of rainforest trees.

**Y** is for Yams. There are more than 150 varieties of yams (similar to sweet potatoes). Yams are a primary agricultural crop in West Africa and New Guinea. They can grow up to 7 feet (2 m) long and weigh as much as 150 pounds (68 kg). They are a food staple for many rainforest peoples.

Yy

Scientists estimate that there are about 10 million species of plants, animals, and insects throughout the world. Interestingly, more than 5 million species (most undiscovered) live in tropical rainforests. Consider these facts:

- The number of fish species in the Amazon exceeds the number in the entire Atlantic Ocean.

- A single 25-acre (10 ha) section of rainforest in Southeast Asia can have more than 700 species of trees.

- Twenty percent of all the birds in the world live in the Amazon rainforest.

- At least 3,000 varieties of fruits grow in the rainforests of the world.

- More than 430,000 species of plants have been discovered in the Amazon rainforest—with many more that remain to be discovered.

- Scientists have estimated that a single hectare (2.47 acres) of Amazon rainforest contains about 900 tons of living plants.

- Seventy percent of the plants used to produce drugs that fight cancer come from the rainforest.

- By some estimates at least one and a half acres (about a half hectare) of rainforest are lost every second of every day.

Z is for the number Zero.
I hope you'll understand—
it's all the species that are left,
if we don't preserve this land.

Zz

Some experts estimate that more than 130 plant, animal, and insect species are lost every single day due to rainforest deforestation (that's about 50,000 species a year)! If deforestation continues at current rates, some scientists figure that nearly 80 to 90 percent of tropical rainforest ecosystems may be destroyed within the next 25 years.

# Q & A The Rainforest Way!

1. What animal spends most of its life upside down?

2. What group of rainforest people have no written language?

3. How many prescription drugs have their origin in rainforest plants?

4. How many gorillas do scientists estimate are left in the wild?

5. What is the layer of the rainforest where most of the plants and animals live?

6. What tree is known for its large buttresses?

7. What type of plants do not need soil to grow and thrive?

8. The average tropical rainforest gets how many inches (cm) of rain a year?

9. What rainforest plant do we use to flavor our ice cream?

10. What is the largest country in South America?

### Answers

1. The two-toed or three-toed sloth
2. Yanomamo
3. More than 100
4. 50,000
5. The canopy layer
6. Kapok tree
7. Epiphytes
8. 80 (200 cm)
9. Vanilla
10. Brazil

## Tony Fredericks

Tony Fredericks grew up in Newport Beach, California, where he surfed, skate-boarded, and played beach volleyball almost every day. He now lives on a wooded hillside in south-central Pennsylvania where his neighbors include furry creatures, slithering reptiles, and some (very smart) squirrels who are always robbing the bird feeder. He is an award-winning children's author of nearly three dozen nature and animal books as well as the popular Sleeping Bear Press book, *The Tsunami Quilt: Grandfather's Story*. He is also an enthusiastic and energetic visiting author to elementary schools throughout the U.S. Tony teaches education courses at York College in York, PA. He is a frequent traveler to the rainforests of Hawai'i and Central America.

## Laura Regan

Laura Regan, born in Canada and raised in California, studied graphic design at the Maryland Institute College of Art, but soon found that painting was her true passion. She began illustrating books in 1990 after hearing that school children were captivated by an exhibit of her exotic wildlife paintings, particularly those with creatures from the rainforest. She has illustrated several award-winning books and has used her art to help raise funds for various wildlife organizations. Laura lives near San Francisco with her husband. Together they have six grown children.